SIMPLY THE BEST
QUADCHOP RECIPES
MARIAN GETZ

INTRODUCTION BY WOLFGANG PUCK

Copyright © 2014 Marian Getz

A most sincere thank you to our wonderful viewers and customers for without you there would be no need for a cookbook. I try very hard to give you an array of recipes suited for the particular kitchen tool the cookbook is written for. Wolfgang and I create recipes faster than we can write them down. That is what chefs do and is also the reason to tune in to the live shows and even record them so you can learn new dishes that may not be in our cookbooks yet.

Thank you most of all to Wolfgang. You are the most passionate chef I know and it has been a privilege to work for you since 1998. You are a great leader and friend. Your restaurants are full of cooks and staff that have been with you for 20 or more years which is a true testament to how you lead us. Thanks for allowing me to write these cookbooks and for letting me share the stage at HSN with you.

To Greg, my sweet husband since 1983. Working together is a dream and I love you. You have taught me what a treasure it is to have a home filled with people to laugh with.

To my sons, Jordan and Ben, we have a beautiful life, don't we? It just keeps on getting better since we added Lindsay, J. J., precious Easton and our second grand baby Sadie Lynn.

To all the great people at WP Productions, Syd, Arnie, Mike, Phoebe, Michael, Nicolle, Tracy, Genevieve, Gina, Nancy, Sylvain and the rest of the team, you are all amazing to work with. Watching all the wonderful items we sell develop from idea to final product on live television is an awe-inspiring process to see and I love that I get to be a part of it.

To Daniel Koren, our patient editor and photographer, thank you for your dedication. You make the photo shoot days fun and you are such an easygoing person to work with in the cramped, hot studio we have to share. We have learned so much together and have far more to learn.

To Greg, Cat, Estela, Angi, Laurie, Keith, Marible, Maria and Margarita who are the most dedicated, loving staff anyone could wish for. You are the true heroes behind the scenes. You are a well-oiled machine of very hard working people who pull off the live shows at HSN. It is a magical production to watch, from the first box unpacked, to the thousands of eggs cracked and beaten to running to get that "thing" Wolf asks for at the last minute, to the very last dish washed and put away it is quite a sight to behold. I love you all and I deeply love what we do.

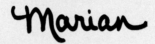

The modern tools we have in the kitchen, whether in the restaurant or at home, are expected to be able to do more than one thing. While a chopper is typically thought of as an appliance that can only chop ingredients, the QuadChop is capable of performing a variety of tasks. This kitchen tool can be used to make breakfast, lunch, dinner, sauces, dressings, drinks and more.

The QuadChop is the perfect multi-tasker. The different speed buttons and multiple blades allow for doing anything from roughly chopping ingredients to smoothly blending milkshakes.

Marian's "Simply The Best QuadChop Recipes" cookbook is the perfect match for my QuadChop. She has done an amazing job at writing recipes that will even make a novice cook fell like a pro. Over the years, Marian has proven to me to be a very reliable resource. I admire her experience in the kitchen, both in the restaurant and at home. While she likes making challenging dishes, she is also comfortable preparing everyday meals that her family loves to eat. The QuadChop is the perfect kitchen helper for making both, which lead her to write this cookbook.

As I learned long ago, alongside my mother and grandmother, you should always put lots of love into everything you cook. This is certainly evident in this cookbook.

Wolfgang Puck

INTRODUCTION BY WOLFGANG PUCK

TABLE OF CONTENTS

RECIPES

TABLE OF CONTENTS

QUADCHOP TIPS

Most recipes start with chopped up vegetables such as onions and garlic. The QuadChop dramatically cuts down your meal prep time, allowing you to cook more often for your family, even with an already busy schedule. Just pop your ingredients into the QuadChop then tap away on the desired speed button and watch your ingredients chop effortlessly in seconds to make anything from drinks to dinner to dessert. Here are some tips to help you achieve the best results:

ADDING INGREDIENTS

It may be necessary to cut some ingredients into smaller pieces to fit into the QuadChop bowl. As a general rule, if the ingredient fits between the shaft and the side wall of the QuadChop bowl, it does not need to be cut into smaller pieces before chopping. The exception are very hard ingredients such as Parmesan cheese.

OVERFILLING

Do not fill the QuadChop bowl more than 1/2 full of ingredients or they will not get chopped evenly. If you overfill the QuadChop bowl, the ingredients at the bottom will get chopped faster than the top ingredients, resulting in inconsistent chopping of the QuadChop bowl contents.

CHOPPING IN BATCHES

Some ingredients can vary greatly in size and shape. It may be necessary for you to chop ingredients in batches, even though it is not stated in the recipe. For example, fruits and vegetables purchased at a big club store can be up to twice as large as their regular grocery store counterpart. While this will normally not affect the outcome of a recipe, it might mean that you will need to take the extra step and chop the ingredients in batches.

OVERMIXING

Watch closely when using your QuadChop as its fast speed can potentially overmix your ingredients. To monitor the progress during chopping, it's best to tilt your head and view the QuadChop bowl from eye level then stop chopping when desired consistency is achieved.

SPEED SETTINGS

The difference between the HIGH and LOW button of your QuadChop is the speed at which the blades turn. Start by using the LOW speed until you get a feel for how the QuadChop operates. Once you are comfortable, start using the HIGH speed. As you become more familiar with the appliance, you will most likely use the HIGH speed for the majority of recipes.

CLEANING

For easier cleanup, use a small brush similar to those created for cleaning baby bottles. It is a very helpful tool to remove even the smallest seeds. For general cleaning, I suggest adding 2 inches of warm water to the QuadChop with a small amount of dish washing detergent. Cover and blend on LOW to let the power of the QuadChop do the cleaning for you then rinse with clean water.

COOKING TIPS

HAVE ALL INGREDIENTS READY
Gather all ingredients that a recipe calls for before you begin preparing the recipe. This will help save a significant amount of time in the kitchen.

RAW MEAT
When cooking raw meat, be mindful of what you do with your tongs.
If you use the same pair of tongs to place raw chicken into a pan then later use them to transfer the cooked chicken to a platter, there is a chance that those tongs may still have live bacteria on them. Either wash them before removing cooked food or use a second pair.

KNOW YOUR BUTCHER
If you like to cook but are as busy as I am, I suggest you find a grocery store that still has a real butcher on premise. Make friends with your butcher as a good butcher will save you prep time in the kitchen and make you a better cook because of it. I have my butcher's phone number on speed dial in my phone.

SEASONING YOUR FOOD
When cooking savory foods, it is important to season it first.
It can be as simple as salt alone or an elaborate array of spices and herbs. Season EVERY BITE of the food by sprinkling the seasonings evenly over the surface of the food. For me, salt and pepper do not always go together. Salt is by far the most important seasoning followed by something tart such as citrus, vinegar, wine, BBQ sauce or mustard that has a tartness to it. It's all about the right balance.

PREP ONCE - USE TWICE
Think about any meals you may want to cook during the upcoming week and chop for more than you need today. For example, if you're chopping onions for today's meal, can you use the onions later in the week? If so, prep extra today and save time tomorrow.

SALT

The salt used in this book is Diamond Crystal Kosher Salt. It is half as salty as most other brands. This is because the grains are very fluffy and therefore not as many fit into a measuring spoon. This brand also lists only "salt" as the ingredient on the box. If you are using salt other than Diamond Crystal Kosher Salt, simply use half the amount specified in the recipe.

OIL AND BUTTER

Canola is my favorite neutral-tasting oil and I also like to use olive oil. Try to avoid using extra-virgin olive oil as it has a lower smoke point. High temperatures will ruin its unique fruity flavor. Peanut oil is also a great oil to use if you are not allergic to it. If a recipe calls for butter, I always use the unsalted kind. Salted butter has a longer shelf life as the salt acts as a preservative but it comes at the expense of a taste that is stale compared to that of unsalted butter. Softened butter means butter that has been left at room temperature for several hours. It should be soft enough to offer no resistance whatsoever when sliced using a knife. While there is no perfect substitute for the pure flavor of butter, you can use a substitute such as margarine and most of the recipes will turn out fairly well.

VANILLA

I adore vanilla and order both my vanilla extract and vanilla beans from a supplier directly from the island of Tahiti. I use both of these in recipes where the vanilla flavor takes center stage. In recipes where vanilla is not the star flavor, I use imitation vanilla because it is less expensive and adds the right amount of taste and aroma without overpowering the other flavors. My favorite is an inexpensive imitation flavoring called Magic Line Butter Vanilla Extract. It adds an incredible sweet smell and taste to baked goods.

CHOCOLATE

Buy good quality chocolate and cocoa whenever possible. It is easy to find excellent chocolate at most grocery stores but it is almost impossible to find good quality cocoa powder. I suggest ordering it online.

SUGAR SUBSTITUTE

If you need to use a sugar substitute, my favorite kind is an all-natural product called Zsweet. I get it at my local health food store. While it does not bake as perfectly as regular sugar, it is the best substitute I know. I also like agave and stevia.

PANTRY TIPS

Being prepared to cook the recipes in this book, or any recipe for that matter, is one of the keys to success in the kitchen. Your pantry must be stocked with the basics. We all know how frustrating it can be when you go to the cupboard and what you need is not there. This list includes some of the ingredients you will find in this book and some that we feel are important to always have on hand.

PERISHABLES:

Onions
Garlic
Tomatoes
Carrots
Celery
Ginger
Bell Peppers
White Potatoes
Sweet Potatoes
Squashes
Citrus
Apples
Bananas
Lettuce
Spinach
Fresh Herbs
Green Onions
Milk
Cream Cheese
Parmesan Cheese
Yogurt
Other Cheeses You Like

SPICES:

Kosher Salt
Pepper
Bay Leaves
Sage
Oregano
Thyme
Chili Flakes
Cumin Seeds
Curry Powder
Onion Powder
Garlic Powder
Dry Mustard
Ground Cinnamon
Nutmeg
Cloves
Chili Powder

DRY GOODS:

Sugars
Sugar Substitute
Vanilla
Extracts/Flavorings
Agave Syrup
Canned Tomatoes
Canned Beans
Canned Vegetables
Dried Chilies
Pasta
Lentils
Stocks
Powdered Bouillon
Olives
Ketchup
Mustard
Pickles
Oils
Vinegar
Honey

It is not necessary to have all the items listed at all times. However, if you are feeling creative, adventurous or just following a recipe, it's great to have a good selection in the kitchen.

DUTCH BABY PANCAKE

Makes 2-4 servings

Ingredients:

3/4 cup whole milk
3 large eggs
3/4 cup all purpose flour
1/4 teaspoon kosher salt
3 tablespoons unsalted butter
2 cups mixed berries
Maple syrup and powdered sugar, for serving

Method:

1. *Fit QuadChop bowl with blades then add the milk, eggs, flour and salt.*
2. *Cover with lid and place motor on top; pulse on HIGH for 10-15 seconds or until smooth.*
3. *Place an oven-safe 12-inch omelet pan in the oven and preheat oven to 450°F.*
4. *When oven is preheated, carefully remove the pan then add the butter to the hot pan and swirl to melt using a pot holder or oven mitt.*
5. *Pour the batter into the center of the omelet pan then return the pan to the oven.*
6. *Bake for 25-30 minutes or until deep brown and dramatically puffed into a bowl shape.*
7. *Remove to a trivet then top with berries, syrup and powdered sugar and serve immediately.*

CHICKEN SALAD

Makes 4 servings

Ingredients:

1/2 celery stalk
1/4 cup walnuts, toasted
1/4 Golden Delicious apple, cored
3 cups cooked chicken, skinless and boneless
1/4 medium red onion
1/4 cup raisins
1/4 cup red grapes, seedless
2 tablespoons jarred sweet relish
1/2 cup mayonnaise
1 tablespoon yellow mustard
1 teaspoon kosher salt
1/2 teaspoon fresh black pepper
1/2 teaspoon fresh lemon juice
1/2 teaspoon celery seeds
1 teaspoon bottled hot pepper sauce

Method:

1. *Fit QuadChop bowl with blades then add the celery, walnuts and apple.*
2. *Cover with lid and place motor on top; pulse on HIGH for 5-10 seconds or until chunky.*
3. *Transfer mixture to a large bowl then repeat with cooked chicken and pulse to desired texture.*
4. *Transfer the chicken to the large bowl.*
5. *Place remaining ingredients into the QuadChop bowl.*
6. *Cover with lid and place motor on top; pulse on LOW for 10-15 seconds or until chunky.*
7. *Transfer QuadChop contents to the large bowl and stir gently to combine before serving.*
8. *Keep refrigerated in an airtight container for up to 2 days.*

PISTACHIO FRENCH TOAST

Makes 4 servings

For the French Toast:
1 1/2 cups pistachio nuts, divided
6 large eggs
1/2 teaspoon pure vanilla extract
2 cups heavy cream
1 loaf brioche or challah, cut into 8 equal slices

For Serving:
Butter
Maple syrup
Powdered sugar

Method:

1. *Fit QuadChop bowl with blades then add half of the pistachio nuts.*
2. *Cover with lid and place motor on top; pulse on HIGH for 5-10 seconds or until coarsely ground.*
3. *Remove and repeat with remaining nuts then transfer to a shallow bowl.*
4. *Pour the eggs, vanilla and heavy cream into the QuadChop bowl.*
5. *Cover with lid and place motor on top; pulse on HIGH for 5-10 seconds or until smooth.*
6. *Transfer egg mixture to a separate shallow bowl.*
7. *Preheat a large skillet or griddle over medium heat.*
8. *Dip each bread slice on both sides first into the egg mixture then dip one side of each slice into the ground pistachio nuts.*
9. *Apply nonstick cooking spray to the skillet or griddle then add bread slices, nut-side up, and cook for 3 minutes or until golden brown.*
10. *Flip and cook for an additional 2 minutes then remove and repeat with any remaining bread slices.*
11. *Serve with desired toppings.*

TIP

It is important to use nuts that have not been toasted in this recipe as they get toasted during cooking.

EASY DEVILED EGGS

Makes 16 eggs

Ingredients:

12 hard boiled eggs, shells removed
1/2 cup mayonnaise
2 teaspoons yellow mustard
2 tablespoons sweet pickle relish
1 teaspoon kosher salt
1/2 teaspoon granulated sugar
1/8 teaspoon cayenne pepper
2 teaspoons cider vinegar
Paprika, for garnish

Method:

1. *Cut eggs in half lengthwise then remove the egg yolks; set aside.*
2. *Rinse the egg white halves, wrap them in plastic wrap and chill until ready to fill.*
3. *Fit QuadChop bowl with blades then add the egg yolks and remaining ingredients, except egg white halves and paprika.*
4. *Cover with lid and place motor on top; press and hold HIGH for 10-15 seconds or until smooth.*
5. *Taste and adjust seasoning if desired.*
6. *Transfer egg mixture to a pastry bag and pipe mixture into the egg whites halves.*
7. *Sprinkle with paprika then cover and chill until ready to serve.*

SPINACH & POTATO
FRITTATA

Makes 2 - 3 servings

Ingredients:

1/2 of a small yellow onion
4 Red Bliss potatoes
3 green onions, quartered
1 garlic clove
1 cup fresh spinach
Kosher salt and fresh pepper to taste
6 large eggs
1/2 cup Parmesan cheese, grated
2 tablespoons olive oil

Method:

1. *Fit QuadChop bowl with blades then add all ingredients, except olive oil.*
2. *Cover with lid and place motor on top; pulse on LOW for 5-10 seconds or until chunky.*
3. *Preheat the oil in a large 12-inch skillet over medium-high heat.*
4. *Transfer the egg mixture from the QuadChop bowl to the skillet and stir gently.*
5. *Reduce heat to low, cover and cook for 3-5 minutes or until eggs are set.*
6. *Remove from pan, garnish as desired and serve immediately.*

ONE POT BEEF & MUSHROOMS

Makes 4-6 servings

Ingredients:

1 large yellow onion, quartered
4 garlic cloves
1 carrot, chunked
1 celery stalk, chunked
1 pound lean ground beef
1 package (4 ounces) sliced mushrooms
2 1/2 cups dry rotini pasta
2 1/2 cups beef stock
1 jar (20 ounces) pasta sauce
Kosher salt and fresh pepper to taste
1 bag (10 ounces) frozen green beans

Method:

1. *Fit QuadChop bowl with blades then add the onions, garlic, carrots and celery.*
2. *Cover with lid and place motor on top; pulse on HIGH for 5-10 seconds or until roughly chopped.*
3. *Transfer QuadChop bowl contents and beef to a large skillet over medium-high heat; stir.*
4. *Cook for 4-6 minutes or until vegetables and beef are slightly cooked.*
5. *Add remaining ingredients, except green beans, to the skillet; stir thoroughly.*
6. *Cover skillet then reduce heat to medium and cook for 8 minutes; stir.*
7. *Add the green beans to the skillet; cover again and cook for an additional 8 minutes, stirring occasionally to prevent sticking.*
8. *Remove from heat and serve.*

SKILLET CHEESEBURGER SUPPER

Makes 4-6 servings

Ingredients:

1 tablespoon vegetable oil
1 large yellow onion, quartered
1 pound beef stew meat
2 1/2 cups dry wagon wheel pasta
2 1/2 cups beef stock
1/2 cup ketchup
1/4 cup yellow mustard
1/4 cup mayonnaise
Kosher salt and fresh pepper to taste
2 dill pickles, thinly sliced
1 1/2 cups Cheddar cheese, shredded

Method:

1. *Fit QuadChop bowl with blades then add the oil and onions.*
2. *Cover with lid and place motor on top; pulse on HIGH for 5-10 seconds or until roughly chopped.*
3. *Transfer QuadChop bowl contents to a large skillet over medium-high heat; stir.*
4. *Add the meat to the QuadChop bowl.*
5. *Cover with lid and place motor on top; pulse on HIGH for 10-15 seconds or until ground.*
6. *Add QuadChop bowl contents to the skillet.*
7. *Cook for 4-6 minutes or until ground meat is mostly brown and crumbled.*
8. *Add remaining ingredients, except cheese, to the skillet; stir thoroughly.*
9. *Cover skillet then reduce heat to medium and cook for 8 minutes.*
10. *Remove lid, stir then cover again and cook for an additional 8 minutes, stirring occasionally to prevent sticking.*
11. *Remove from heat, stir in the cheese and serve.*

HERBED PIZZA BREAD

Makes 4-6 servings

For the Pizza Bread:
1/2 cup + 2 tablespoons water, room temperature
1 envelope dry active yeast
2 tablespoons honey
1 1/2 cups all purpose flour
1 teaspoon kosher salt
1 tablespoon vegetable oil
2 tablespoons unsalted butter, melted

Toppings:
1 teaspoon kosher salt
2 tablespoons fresh sage leaves, torn
1/4 red onion, thinly sliced
1 teaspoon dried Italian seasoning
1/4 cup green olives, sliced

Method:

1. *Fit QuadChop bowl with blades then add all pizza bread ingredients, except butter.*
2. *Cover with lid and place motor on top; press and hold HIGH for 10-15 seconds or until a smooth and wet dough forms.*
3. *Pour half of the melted butter onto a small sheet pan and spread it around.*
4. *Pour the dough onto the sheet pan then top with remaining butter.*
5. *Pat and pull dough to fit the shape of the sheet pan then let rest for 30 minutes.*
6. *Preheat oven to 400°F.*
7. *Dimple the top of the dough all over using your fingers then let rest for 5 minutes.*
8. *Top dough with topping ingredients and bake for 20 minutes or until puffed and brown (rotate sheet pan halfway after 10 minutes of baking).*
9. *Remove, cut into wedges and serve hot.*

EASY BISCUITS

Makes 8 biscuits

Ingredients:

1 cup all purpose flour
2 teaspoons granulated sugar
1 1/2 teaspoons baking powder
1/4 teaspoon kosher salt
3/4 cup heavy cream

Method:

1. *Preheat oven to 375°F.*
2. *Line a cookie sheet with parchment paper.*
3. *Fit QuadChop bowl with blades then add all ingredients.*
4. *Cover with lid and place motor on top; press and hold HIGH for 10-15 seconds or until a dough ball forms.*
5. *Using a small ice cream scoop, drop the biscuit dough 1-inch apart onto the cookie sheet.*
6. *Pat down the tops using your fingers.*
7. *Bake for 15-17 minutes or until golden brown and puffed.*
8. *Remove and serve hot.*

TIP

If you like biscuits with soft sides, drop the biscuit dough onto the cookie sheet almost touching each other instead of 1-inch apart.

Marian's Fresh Strawberry Jelly

POTATO & LEEK SOUP

Makes 6 servings

Ingredients:

3 medium Russet potatoes, peeled and quartered
3 cups leeks, rinsed and chunked
2 quarts water
1 tablespoon kosher salt
1/3 cup heavy cream

Method:

1. *Fit QuadChop bowl with blades then add half of the potatoes and leeks.*
2. *Cover with lid and place motor on top; pulse on HIGH for 10-15 seconds or until fine.*
3. *Transfer QuadChop bowl contents to an 8-quart stockpot then repeat with remaining potatoes and leeks.*
4. *Add QuadChop bowl contents and remaining ingredients to the stockpot and simmer for 30 minutes over low heat.*
5. *Ladle into bowls, garnish as desired and serve.*

SWISS STEAK

Makes 4- 6 servings

Ingredients:

2 large yellow onions, quartered
1 medium bell pepper, quartered
1 carrot, chunked
1 celery stalk, chunked
1 can (28 ounces) stewed tomatoes
1 tablespoon powdered beef bouillon
Kosher salt and fresh pepper to taste
6 cubed steaks (5 ounces each)
Hot cooked noodles, for serving

Method:

1. *Fit QuadChop bowl with blades then add the onions, bell peppers, carrots and celery.*
2. *Cover with lid and place motor on top; pulse on HIGH for 5-10 seconds or until chunky.*
3. *Transfer QuadChop bowl contents and remaining ingredients, except noodles, to a large oven-safe Dutch oven or lidded skillet and stir.*
4. *Cover Dutch oven or skillet and place in the cold oven.*
5. *Set oven temperature to 325ºF and bake for 2 1/2 hours or until meat is very tender.*
6. *Remove, garnish as desired and serve over noodles.*

CORN CHOWDER

Makes 5 servings

Ingredients:

1 large yellow onion, quartered
5 ears of corn, kernels removed
6 tablespoons unsalted butter
1/4 cup all purpose flour
1 teaspoon kosher salt
6 cups chicken stock
3 cups Russet potatoes, peeled and finely diced
1 tablespoon granulated sugar
2 teaspoons fresh lemon juice
1/8 teaspoon cayenne pepper
1 cup half & half

Method:

1. *Fit QuadChop bowl with blades then add the onions.*
2. *Cover with lid and place motor on top; pulse on HIGH for 10-15 seconds or until fine.*
3. *Remove the onions from the QuadChop bowl then repeat with the corn kernels.*
4. *Preheat the butter in a stockpot over medium heat until butter is melted.*
5. *Add the onions and corn to the stockpot and simmer for 3 minutes, stirring occasionally.*
6. *Stir in the flour and salt; cook for an additional 3 minutes.*
7. *Add remaining ingredients to the stockpot and simmer for 20 minutes or until potatoes are tender.*
8. *Ladle into bowls, garnish as desired and serve.*

YORKSHIRE PUDDING

Makes 6 servings

Ingredients:
3/4 cup whole milk
3 large eggs
1 tablespoon fresh chives, snipped
3/4 teaspoon kosher salt
3/4 cup all purpose flour
6 teaspoons vegetable oil

TIP

For a more savory Yorkshire pudding, try adding 4 whole garlic cloves to the recipe in step 3. You can also add some herbs such as rosemary, sage or thyme.

Method:

1. *Preheat oven to 400°F.*
2. *Move a rack to the lower part of the oven and place an empty cookie sheet on the rack to catch any drippings.*
3. *Fit QuadChop bowl with blades then add all ingredients, except oil.*
4. *Cover with lid and place motor on top; pulse on HIGH for 5-10 seconds or until smooth.*
5. *Drop 1 teaspoon oil into each well of a 6-cup muffin tin.*
6. *Place the muffin tin on the center rack of the oven and let heat for 5 minutes.*
7. *Open the oven door and carefully fill each muffin well with batter until 2/3 full.*
8. *Bake for 30 minutes or until the puddings are deep brown in color and have risen a few inches above the muffin tin.*
9. *Remove and serve immediately before the puddings deflate.*

GREEN PEA SOUP

Makes 4 servings

Ingredients:

1 large yellow onion, quartered
3 cups frozen peas, thawed
4 sprigs fresh mint
3 cups vegetables stock
1 tablespoon honey
2 teaspoons fresh lemon juice
2 tablespoons heavy cream
Kosher salt and fresh pepper to taste

Method:

1. *Fit QuadChop bowl with blades then add half of the onions, peas and mint.*
2. *Cover with lid and place motor on top; press and hold HIGH for 10-15 seconds or until fine.*
3. *Pour chopped vegetables into the stockpot then repeat with remaining onions, peas and mint.*
4. *Transfer QuadChop bowl contents to the stockpot then add remaining ingredients to the stockpot; bring to a boil over high heat.*
5. *Reduce heat to a simmer then cook for 5 minutes or until smooth in texture.*
6. *Serve in bowls garnished as desired.*

MASHED CAULIFLOWER

Makes 4 servings

Ingredients:

1 small yellow onion, quartered
1 head cauliflower, roughly chopped
2 tablespoons unsalted butter
2 teaspoons honey
1/2 cup heavy cream
Kosher salt and fresh pepper to taste

Method:

1. Fit QuadChop bowl with blades then add the onions and cauliflower.
2. Cover with lid and place motor on top; pulse on HIGH for 10-15 seconds or until fine.
3. Scrape onion mixture into a large saucepot then add remaining ingredients.
4. Simmer over medium heat for 5 minutes, stirring often.
5. Taste and adjust seasoning then garnish as desired before serving.

BACON & ALFREDO PASTA

Makes 4-6 servings

Ingredients:

1 large yellow onion, quartered
4 garlic cloves
1 carrot, chunked
1 celery stalk, chunked
4 slices bacon, diced
2 1/2 cups dry linguini pasta
2 1/2 cups half & half
1/2 cup dry white wine
1 cup Parmesan cheese, grated
Kosher salt and fresh pepper to taste
1 bag (10 ounces) frozen green peas

Method:

1. *Fit QuadChop bowl with blades then add the onions, garlic, carrots and celery.*
2. *Cover with lid and place motor on top; pulse on HIGH for 5-10 seconds or until roughly chopped.*
3. *Transfer QuadChop bowl contents and bacon to a large skillet over medium-high heat; stir.*
4. *Cook for 4-6 minutes or until vegetables and bacon are slightly cooked.*
5. *Add remaining ingredients, except green peas, to the skillet; stir thoroughly.*
6. *Cover skillet then reduce heat to medium and cook for 8 minutes; stir.*
7. *Add the peas to the skillet; cover again and cook for an additional 8 minutes, stirring occasionally to prevent sticking.*
8. *Remove from heat and serve.*

SKILLET BEEF & PASTA SUPPER

Makes 4-6 servings

Ingredients:

1 large yellow onion, quartered
4 garlic cloves
1 carrot, chunked
1 celery stalk, chunked
1 pound cubed steak, cut into 1-inch pieces
2 1/2 cups dry rotini pasta
2 1/2 cups beef stock
1/2 cup dry white wine
1/2 cup whole milk
Kosher salt and fresh pepper to taste
1 package (10 ounces) frozen mushrooms

Method:

1. *Fit QuadChop bowl with blades then add the onions, garlic, carrots and celery.*
2. *Cover with lid and place motor on top; pulse on HIGH for 5-10 seconds or until roughly chopped.*
3. *Transfer QuadChop bowl contents and steak to a large skillet over medium-high heat; stir.*
4. *Cook for 4-6 minutes or until vegetables and steak are slightly cooked.*
5. *Add remaining ingredients, except mushrooms, to the skillet; stir thoroughly.*
6. *Cover skillet then reduce heat to medium and cook for 8 minutes; stir.*
7. *Add the mushrooms to the skillet; cover again and cook for an additional 8 minutes, stirring occasionally to prevent sticking.*
8. *Remove from heat and serve.*

EASY QUADCHOP COLESLAW

Makes 4 servings

Ingredients:

1/4 of a head of cabbage, chunked
1 carrot, chunked
1/2 tart apple, quartered
1 green onion, roughly chopped
1/2 cup mayonnaise
1/4 cup heavy cream
1 tablespoon cider vinegar
2 tablespoons granulated sugar
Kosher salt and fresh pepper to taste

Method:

1. *Fit QuadChop bowl with blades then fill halfway with water and add half of the cabbage, carrots, apples and onions.*
2. *Cover with lid and place motor on top; pulse on HIGH for 10-15 seconds or until fine.*
3. *Pour QuadChop bowl contents into a strainer and repeat with remaining cabbage, carrots, apples and onions.*
4. *Press as much water from the vegetables as possible then transfer to a mixing bowl.*
5. *Add remaining ingredients to the mixing bowl; stir to combine.*
6. *Serve cold.*

DINNER ROLLS

Makes 8 rolls

Ingredients:

1/4 cup water
1 tablespoon sour cream
1 tablespoon unsalted butter, melted
1 teaspoon granulated sugar
1/4 teaspoon kosher salt
1 teaspoon yeast
1 cup all purpose flour

Method:

1. *Fit QuadChop bowl with blades then add all ingredients.*
2. *Cover with lid and place motor on top; pulse on HIGH for 10-15 seconds or until a dough ball forms.*
3. *Let dough ball rest in the QuadChop bowl for 20 minutes then pulse on LOW for an additional 10-15 seconds.*
4. *Remove dough to a floured surface and divide into 8 pieces; roll into balls.*
5. *Arrange evenly, seam-side down, on a greased sheet pan; cover and let rise for 30 minutes.*
6. *Preheat oven to 350°F then bake for 20-25 minutes or until golden brown.*
7. *Remove and serve piping hot.*

BACON & CHEESE FRITTATA

Makes 2-3 servings

Ingredients:

3 green onions, quartered
1 garlic clove
4 strips raw bacon, chunked
Kosher salt and fresh pepper to taste
6 large eggs
1/2 cup sharp Cheddar cheese, grated
2 tablespoons olive oil

TIP
For a delightful twist, substitute 1/2 cup blue cheese for the Cheddar cheese.

Method:

1. *Fit QuadChop bowl with blades then add all ingredients, except olive oil.*
2. *Cover with lid and place motor on top; pulse on LOW for 5-10 seconds or until chunky.*
3. *Preheat the oil in a large 12-inch skillet over medium-high heat.*
4. *Add the egg mixture to the skillet and stir gently.*
5. *Reduce heat to low, cover and cook for 3-5 minutes or until eggs are set.*
6. *Remove from skillet, garnish as desired and serve immediately.*

TURKEY WITH BOW-TIE PASTA

Makes 4-6 servings

Ingredients:

1 large yellow onion, quartered
1 small carrot, quartered
1 celery stalk, quartered
2 garlic cloves
1 pound ground turkey
1 teaspoon dry sage
2 1/2 cups dry bow-tie pasta
2 1/2 cups chicken stock
1/2 cup dry white wine
1/2 cup cranberry sauce (optional)
1/2 cup half & half
Kosher salt and fresh pepper to taste
1 bag (10 ounces) frozen mixed vegetables
1 cup Parmesan cheese, grated

Method:

1. *Fit QuadChop bowl with blades then add the onions, carrots, celery and garlic.*
2. *Cover with lid and place motor on top; pulse on HIGH for 5-10 seconds or until roughly chopped.*
3. *Transfer QuadChop bowl contents and turkey to a large skillet over medium-high heat; stir.*
4. *Cook for 4-6 minutes or until turkey is mostly brown and crumbled.*
5. *Add remaining ingredients, except mixed vegetables and cheese, to the skillet; stir thoroughly.*
6. *Cover skillet then reduce heat to medium and cook for 8 minutes; stir.*
7. *Add the mixed vegetables to the skillet; cover again and cook for an additional 8 minutes, stirring occasionally to prevent sticking.*
8. *Remove from heat, stir in the cheese and serve.*

ONE SKILLET
CHICKEN & RICE

Makes 4-6 servings

Ingredients:

1 tablespoon vegetable oil
1 large yellow onion, quartered
1 small carrot, quartered
1 celery stalk, quartered
2 garlic cloves
3 chicken breasts, quartered
1 1/4 cups long-grain white rice, uncooked
2 1/2 cups chicken stock
1 package (4 ounces) cream cheese, softened
1 teaspoon dry poultry seasoning
Kosher salt and fresh pepper to taste
1 bag (10 ounces) frozen green beans
1/2 cup Parmesan cheese, grated
1/2 cup mozzarella cheese, grated

Method:

1. *Fit QuadChop bowl with blades then add the oil, onions, carrots, celery and garlic.*
2. *Cover with lid and place motor on top; pulse on HIGH for 5-10 seconds or until roughly chopped.*
3. *Transfer QuadChop bowl contents to a large skillet over medium-high heat; stir.*
4. *Add the chicken to the QuadChop bowl.*
5. *Cover with lid and place motor on top; pulse on HIGH for 10-15 seconds or until roughly chopped.*
6. *Add QuadChop bowl contents to the skillet.*
7. *Cook for 4-6 minutes or until chicken is white with bits of brown.*
8. *Add remaining ingredients, except green beans and cheeses, to the skillet; stir thoroughly.*
9. *Cover skillet then reduce heat to medium and cook for 8 minutes; stir.*
10. *Add the green beans to the skillet; cover again and cook for an additional 8 minutes, stirring occasionally to prevent sticking.*
11. *Remove from heat, stir in cheeses and serve.*

CITRUS SLUSHY

Makes 2 servings

Ingredients:

1 cup fresh orange juice
1/4 orange with skin (optional)
1/4 cup fresh grapefruit juice
1 tablespoon fresh lemon juice
1 tablespoon granulated sugar
1 1/2 cups ice cubes
8 Mandarin orange segments
2 lime wedges, for garnish (optional)

Method:

1. *Fit QuadChop bowl with blades then add all ingredients, except Mandarin orange segments and lime wedges.*
2. *Cover with lid and place motor on top; press and hold HIGH for 10-15 seconds or until smooth.*
3. *Place 4 Mandarin orange segments into the bottom of 2 glasses.*
4. *Divide slushy between the glasses then garnish with lime wedges and serve immediately.*

COFFEE MILKSHAKE

Makes 2 servings

Ingredients:

4 scoops vanilla ice cream
1/2 cup half & half
1/4 cup strong coffee, cold
2 teaspoons instant coffee powder

Method:

1. *Fit QuadChop bowl with blades then add all ingredients.*
2. *Cover with lid and place motor on top; press and hold HIGH for 10-15 seconds or until smooth.*
3. *Pour into glasses and serve immediately.*

TIP

A great way to always have instant coffee on hand is to purchase the single serve packets that are readily available at any grocery store from most coffee brands.

BUTTERNUT SQUASH SOUP

Makes 6 servings

Ingredients:

1 large yellow onion, quartered
2 pounds butternut squash, peeled, cut into chunks
2 tablespoons unsalted butter
1 tablespoon olive oil
3 cups chicken stock
Kosher salt and fresh pepper to taste
1 cup half & half or whole milk
1 tablespoon honey
2 teaspoons apple cider vinegar

Method:

1. *Fit QuadChop bowl with blades then add half of the onions and squash.*
2. *Cover with lid and place motor on top; press and hold HIGH for 10-15 seconds or until fine.*
3. *Remove onion-squash mixture from QuadChop bowl then repeat with remaining onions and squash.*
4. *Place the butter and oil into an 8-quart stockpot over medium heat; let heat until butter is melted.*
5. *Add the onion-squash mixture and simmer for 5 minutes, stirring occasionally.*
6. *Add remaining ingredients to the stockpot and simmer for 20 minutes.*
7. *Ladle into bowls, garnish as desired and serve.*

CORN SALSA

Makes 2 cups

Ingredients:

3 ears yellow corn, husks and silk removed
2 Serrano peppers, stems removed
1/2 medium red onion
1/4 red bell pepper, stemmed and seeded
2 tablespoons olive oil
Zest from 1 lime
1/4 cup fresh lime juice
2 teaspoons honey
1 teaspoon fresh oregano leaves
3 garlic cloves
Chipotle-flavored bottled hot sauce, to taste
Handful of fresh cilantro leaves
1/2 teaspoon kosher salt

Method:

1. *On a grill or in a grill pan over medium-high heat, cook the corn and Serrano peppers on all sides until slightly charred; remove and let cool slightly.*
2. *Cut the corn from the cobs into a bowl; set aside.*
3. *Fit QuadChop bowl with blades then add the charred Serrano peppers and remaining ingredients.*
4. *Cover with lid and place motor on top; pulse on HIGH for 10-15 seconds or until chunky.*
5. *Transfer mixture to the bowl with the corn; toss to combine.*
6. *Taste and adjust seasoning if desired before serving.*

TIP

If you are in a pinch, skip the grilling and use frozen corn kernels. It's not exactly the same but still tastes incredible.

WHOLE WHEAT CRACKERS

Makes 6 flatbreads

For the Dough:
2/3 cup water
1 cup all purpose flour
1/2 cup 100% whole wheat flour
1 teaspoon kosher salt

Toppings:
Olive oil
Parmesan cheese, grated
Red onions, thinly sliced
Fresh thyme, or other herbs
Kosher Salt
Freshly cracked pepper
Crushed red pepper flakes

Method:

1. *Preheat oven to 450°F.*
2. *Fit QuadChop bowl with blades then add all dough ingredients.*
3. *Cover with lid and place motor on top; pulse on HIGH for 10-15 seconds or until a dough ball forms.*
4. *Divide the dough into 6 equal balls.*
5. *Using a floured rolling pin, roll out each dough ball as flat as possible.*
6. *Arrange flattened dough disks on 2 sheet pans.*
7. *Brush dough with olive oil then sprinkle with desired toppings (do not put too many toppings on the flatbreads or they will not be crispy).*
8. *Bake for 7-10 minutes or until well browned.*
9. *Remove then top with additional herbs, salt and a drizzle of olive oil before serving.*

TIP

For cheesy crackers, add a 1/4 cup grated Parmesan cheese to the dough ingredients in step 2.

WHITE BEAN DIP

Makes 2 cups

Ingredients:

1 can (15.5 ounces) cannellini beans, drained
2 garlic cloves
1 teaspoon fresh lime zest
Juice from 1 lime
1 green onion, chopped
1 teaspoon soy sauce
4 tablespoons canned chipotle en adobo
1 teaspoon honey
2 tablespoons tomato paste
2 tablespoons vegetable oil
Kosher salt and fresh pepper to taste

Method:

1. *Fit QuadChop bowl with blades then add all ingredients.*
2. *Cover with lid and place motor on top; press and hold HIGH for 10-15 seconds or until smooth.*
3. *Taste and adjust seasoning if desired.*
4. *Keep refrigerated in an airtight container for up to 2 weeks.*

CREAM OF BROCCOLI SOUP

Makes 4-6 servings

Ingredients:

1 large yellow onion, quartered
2 garlic cloves
4 cups broccoli florets
1 medium Russet potato, quartered
Kosher salt and fresh pepper to taste
2 cups vegetable stock
2 cups half & half
2 tablespoons fresh lemon juice
1 tablespoon honey
1/2 cup Cheddar cheese, shredded

Method:

1. Fit QuadChop bowl with blades then add half of the onions, garlic, broccoli and potatoes.
2. Cover with lid and place motor on top; pulse on HIGH for 10-15 seconds or until fine.
3. Scrape into a large saucepot then repeat with remaining onions, garlic, broccoli and potatoes.
4. Add remaining ingredients to the saucepot then simmer over medium heat for 8-10 minutes, stirring often.
5. Garnish as desired before serving.

ONE PAN SAUSAGE & PASTA DINNER

Makes 4-6 servings

Ingredients:

1 large yellow onion, quartered
1 bell pepper, quartered
4 garlic cloves
1 pound sweet Italian sausage
2 1/2 cups dry penne pasta
2 1/2 cups chicken stock
1/2 cup dry white wine
1/2 cup half & half
Kosher salt and fresh pepper to taste
1 bag (10 ounces) frozen broccoli florets
1/2 cup grated Parmesan cheese, for serving
1/2 cup Ricotta cheese, for serving

Method:

1. *Fit QuadChop bowl with blades then add the onions, bell peppers and garlic.*
2. *Cover with lid and place motor on top; pulse on HIGH for 5-10 seconds or until roughly chopped.*
3. *Transfer QuadChop bowl contents and sausage to a large skillet over medium-high heat; stir.*
4. *Cook for 4-6 minutes or until sausage is mostly brown and crumbled.*
5. *Add remaining ingredients, except broccoli and cheeses, to the skillet; stir thoroughly.*
6. *Cover skillet then reduce heat to medium and cook for 8 minutes; stir.*
7. *Add the broccoli to the skillet; cover again and cook for an additional 8 minutes, stirring occasionally to prevent sticking.*
8. *Remove from heat and serve topped with both cheeses.*

SKILLET TUNA & LINGUINI

Makes 4-6 servings

Ingredients:

1 small yellow onion, quartered
1 small carrot, quartered
1 celery stalk, quartered
2 garlic cloves
2 cans (5 ounces each) tuna in water, drained
2 1/2 cups dry linguini pasta, broken into thirds
2 1/2 cups chicken stock
1/2 cup half & half
1 package (4 ounces) cream cheese, softened
Kosher salt and fresh pepper to taste
1 bag (10 ounces) frozen peas and carrot mix
1 cup Parmesan cheese, grated
12 butter-type crackers, crumbled

Method:

1. *Fit QuadChop bowl with blades then add the onions, carrots, celery and garlic.*
2. *Cover with lid and place motor on top; pulse on HIGH for 5-10 seconds or until roughly chopped.*
3. *Transfer QuadChop bowl contents to a large skillet over medium-high heat; stir.*
4. *Add remaining ingredients, except peas and carrot mix, cheese and crackers to the skillet; stir thoroughly.*
5. *Cover skillet then reduce heat to medium-low and cook for 8 minutes; stir.*
6. *Add the peas and carrot mix to the skillet; cover again and cook for an additional 8 minutes, stirring occasionally to prevent sticking.*
7. *Remove from heat, stir in the cheese then serve topped with crumbled crackers.*

PASTA SAUCE WITH CHICKEN

Makes 4-6 servings

Ingredients:

1 large yellow onion, quartered
1 large carrot, chunked
1 celery stalk, roughly chopped
4 garlic cloves
4 boneless, skinless chicken thighs, raw
3 tablespoons tomato paste
2 tablespoons honey
2 cups chicken stock
1 can (28 ounces) tomato puree
1/2 cup dry white wine
1/2 cup heavy cream
Kosher salt and fresh pepper to taste

Method:

1. *Fit QuadChop bowl with blades then add the onions, carrots, celery and garlic.*
2. *Cover with lid and place motor on top; pulse on HIGH for 10-15 seconds or until fine.*
3. *Transfer QuadChop bowl contents into a large saucepot then repeat with the chicken thighs until coarsely ground.*
4. *Scrape ground chicken into the saucepot then add remaining ingredients.*
5. *Bring to a simmer over medium heat then reduce heat to low and simmer for 25 minutes, stirring often.*
6. *Serve as desired.*

CAESAR SALAD DRESSING

Makes about 2 cups

Ingredients:

5 garlic cloves
1/4 small yellow onion
1 tablespoon anchovy paste
1 tablespoon dry mustard powder
1 large egg, preferably pasteurized
Zest and juice of 1 lemon
3 tablespoons red wine vinegar
1/2 teaspoon kosher salt
1/2 teaspoon freshly cracked black pepper
1/2 teaspoon Worcestershire sauce
1 1/4 cups olive oil
1 cup Parmesan cheese, grated

Method:

1. Fit QuadChop bowl with blades then add all ingredients.
2. Cover with lid and place motor on top; pulse on HIGH for 10-15 seconds or until smooth.
3. Use a spatula to scrape the sides of the bowl if needed.
4. Pour into a small serving bowl and use as desired.
5. Keep refrigerated in an airtight container for up to 5 days.

PEANUT DRESSING

Makes about 1 cup

Ingredients:

1/4 cup coconut milk, microwaved until hot
1/2 cup peanut butter, warmed in microwave
1/4 small yellow onion
2 garlic cloves
2 coins fresh ginger
Zest and juice of 1 lime
1 tablespoon honey
1 teaspoon fish sauce or anchovy paste
1 tablespoon soy sauce
Sriracha or other hot sauce, to taste
Chopped peanuts, for garnishing

Method:

1. *Fit QuadChop bowl with blades then add all ingredients, except chopped peanuts.*
2. *Cover with lid and place motor on top; pulse on HIGH for 10-15 seconds or until smooth.*
3. *Use a spatula to scrape the sides of the bowl if needed.*
4. *Pour into a small serving bowl, top with chopped peanuts and use as desired.*
5. *Keep refrigerated in an airtight container for up to 5 days.*

TIP

For a delicious low-fat version, substitute 1/2 cup powdered peanut butter mixed with 1/4 cup water for the regular peanut butter. The powdered peanut butter has 85% less fat and is sold in a 6.5 oz. jar next to the regular peanut butter at the grocery store.

CREAMY AVOCADO DRESSING

Makes about 1 1/4 cups

Ingredients:

1 avocado, peeled and pitted
1 garlic clove
3 green onions, quartered
Zest and juice of 1 lime
2 tablespoons vegetable oil
1/2 cup plain Greek yogurt
3 sprigs fresh cilantro
1/2 teaspoon kosher salt
1/4 teaspoon fresh pepper
A pinch of chili flakes

Method:

1. *Fit QuadChop bowl with blades then add all ingredients.*
2. *Cover with lid and place motor on top; pulse on HIGH for 10-15 seconds or until smooth.*
3. *Use a spatula to scrape the sides of the bowl if needed.*
4. *Pour into a small serving bowl and use as desired.*
5. *Keep refrigerated in an airtight container for up to 2 days.*

CARROT GINGER SOUP

Makes 4 servings

Ingredients:

4 cups carrots, peeled and chunked
1 large yellow onion, quartered
2 coins fresh ginger
Kosher salt and fresh pepper to taste
2 tablespoons honey
1 tablespoon fresh lemon juice
4 cups vegetable stock
2 tablespoons unsalted butter
Fresh herbs, for garnishing

Method:

1. *Fit QuadChop bowl with blades then add half of the carrots, onions and ginger.*
2. *Cover with lid and place motor on top; press and hold HIGH for 10-15 seconds or until fine.*
3. *Transfer QuadChop bowl contents into a stockpot and repeat with remaining carrots, onions and ginger.*
4. *Add remaining ingredients, except fresh herbs for garnishing, to the stockpot and bring to a boil over high heat.*
5. *Reduce heat to low and simmer for 20 minutes or until smooth in texture.*
6. *Serve in bowls garnished with fresh herbs.*

GREEN APPLE & CURRY SALSA

Makes 2 cups

Ingredients:

Juice from 1 lemon
1/8 teaspoon cayenne pepper
1/4 cup fresh flat leaf parsley
1 teaspoon fresh thyme leaves
1 tablespoon curry powder
1 tablespoon maple syrup
2 tablespoons olive oil
Pinch of kosher salt
Pinch of freshly ground black pepper
2 Granny Smith apples, cored and quartered

Method:

1. *Fit QuadChop bowl with blades then add all ingredients, except apples.*
2. *Cover with lid and place motor on top; pulse on HIGH for 5-10 seconds or until roughly chopped.*
3. *Add the apples to the QuadChop bowl and pulse again until apples are roughly chopped.*
4. *Taste and adjust seasoning if desired before serving.*

TIP

For a variation, try using different types of apples such as Pink Lady or Gala.

GREEN GODDESS DRESSING

Makes 1 1/4 cups

Ingredients:

1 garlic clove
1 packed cup of a mixture of tarragon leaves, parsley sprigs, basil leaves and spinach leaves
1 tablespoon dry mustard
2 tablespoons apple cider vinegar
1 anchovy filet
1 teaspoon capers
1 tablespoon granulated sugar
2 teaspoons kosher salt
1/4 teaspoon freshly cracked black pepper
1 cup vegetable oil

Method:

1. *Fit QuadChop bowl with blades then add all ingredients.*
2. *Cover with lid and place motor on top; press and hold HIGH for 10-15 seconds or until mixture begins to thicken.*
3. *Taste and adjust seasoning then use as desired.*
4. *Keep refrigerated in an airtight container for up to 3 days.*

TIP

I love anchovy in some foods but dislike dealing with those oily little anchovy cans. You can substitute the anchovy filet with 1 teaspoon of anchovy paste.

POPPY SEED DRESSING

Makes about 2 cups

Ingredients:

2 tablespoons poppy seeds
1 garlic clove
1 medium yellow onion, quartered
Zest and juice of 1 lemon
1 cup vegetable oil
2 tablespoons apple cider vinegar
1 tablespoon dry mustard powder
1 teaspoon kosher salt
1/3 cup granulated sugar

Method:

1. *Fit QuadChop bowl with blades then add all ingredients.*
2. *Cover with lid and place motor on top; pulse on HIGH for 10-15 seconds or until smooth.*
3. *Use a spatula to scrape the sides of the bowl if needed.*
4. *Pour into a small serving bowl and use as desired.*
5. *Keep refrigerated in an airtight container for up to 1 week.*

PEACH SALSA

Makes 2 cups

Ingredients:

1 pound fresh peaches, peeled and pitted
1/4 medium red onion, peeled and halved
1/3 cup fresh lime juice
1/4 cup peach nectar
1 jalapeño pepper, ribs and seeds removed (or to taste)
1/4 cup fresh cilantro leaves
1/8 cup fresh basil leaves
2 tablespoons fresh mint leaves
1 garlic clove
1/2 teaspoon kosher salt

Method:

1. *Fit QuadChop bowl with blades then add all ingredients.*
2. *Cover with lid and place motor on top; pulse on HIGH for 10-15 seconds until chunky or until desired consistency is achieved.*
3. *Taste and adjust seasoning if desired before serving.*

TIP

For a variation, substitute the peaches with a similarly textured and fragrant fruit like apricots or plums.

CREAMY MICROWAVE ALFREDO SAUCE

Makes 2 servings

Ingredients:

1 cup Parmesan cheese, in small chunks
4 garlic cloves
2 tablespoons dry white wine
1 1/2 cups heavy cream
Kosher salt and fresh pepper to taste

Method:

1. *Fit QuadChop bowl with blades then add the Parmesan cheese and garlic.*
2. *Cover with lid and place motor on top; pulse on HIGH for 5-10 seconds or until chopped.*
3. *Use a spatula to scrape the sides of the bowl then press and hold HIGH for an additional 10-15 seconds.*
4. *Add remaining ingredients to the QuadChop bowl.*
5. *Cover with lid and place motor on top; press and hold HIGH for an additional 10 seconds or until fairly smooth.*
6. *Remove the blades then place the uncovered QuadChop bowl in the microwave.*
7. *Cook in the microwave for 2 minutes, remove, stir then microwave for an additional 1 minute.*
8. *Stir and let stand for 1-2 minutes to thicken.*
9. *Use as desired.*

CREAMY ZUCCHINI SOUP

Makes 4 servings

Ingredients:

5 cups leeks, rinsed and chunked
2 medium Russet potatoes, rinsed and quartered
2 zucchini, chunked
1 tablespoon unsalted butter
1 tablespoon olive oil
6 cups chicken stock
1 teaspoon kosher salt
1/2 teaspoon fresh black pepper
1 tablespoon fresh lemon juice
2 teaspoons honey
1 teaspoon bottled sriracha hot sauce
1/2 cup heavy cream

Method:

1. Fit QuadChop bowl with blades then add half of the leeks, potatoes and zucchini.
2. Cover with lid and place motor on top; press and hold HIGH for 10-15 seconds or until fine.
3. Transfer QuadChop bowl contents to an 8-quart stockpot then repeat with remaining leeks, potatoes and zucchini.
4. Add QuadChop bowl contents and remaining ingredients to the stockpot and simmer over medium heat for 20 minutes.
5. Ladle into bowls, garnish as desired and serve.

ROASTED TOMATO SOUP

Makes 6 servings

Ingredients:

3 pounds ripe plum tomatoes, cut in half lengthwise
1 large yellow onion, quartered
6 garlic cloves
1/4 cup olive oil
1 tablespoon kosher salt
2 teaspoons fresh black pepper
2 tablespoons unsalted butter
1/4 teaspoon crushed red pepper flakes
1 can (28 ounces) tomato puree
1 quart chicken stock or water
6 basil leaves, julienned

Method:

1. Preheat oven to 400°F.
2. In a bowl, combine the plum tomatoes, onions, garlic, olive oil, salt and pepper; toss.
3. Arrange in a single layer on a baking sheet.
4. Roast in the oven for 30 minutes then remove and set aside to cool.
5. Fit QuadChop bowl with blades then add half of the roasted plum tomatoes, onions and garlic.
6. Cover with lid and place motor on top; pulse on HIGH for 10-15 seconds or until fine.
7. Transfer QuadChop bowl contents to an 8-quart stockpot then repeat with remaining roasted plum tomatoes, onions and garlic.
8. Add the QuadChop bowl contents and remaining ingredients, except basil leaves, to the stockpot and simmer for 30 minutes over low heat.
9. Ladle into bowls, garnish with basil leaves and serve.

TOMATO SALSA

Makes 2 cups

Ingredients:

4 small vine-ripened tomatoes
3 plum tomatoes
1/2 medium white onion
2 Serrano peppers, stems and seeds removed (or to taste)
1 garlic clove
1/4 cup fresh cilantro leaves
1 teaspoon kosher salt

Method:

1. *Preheat a sauté or grill pan over medium heat.*
2. *Add the tomatoes, onions, peppers and garlic to the pan.*
3. *Sauté for 5-10 minutes or until the vegetables are slightly charred.*
4. *Fit QuadChop bowl with blades then add the sauté pan contents and remaining ingredients.*
5. *Cover with lid and place motor on top; pulse on HIGH for 10-15 seconds until chunky or until desired consistency.*
6. *Taste and adjust seasoning if desired before serving.*

CILANTRO RICE

Makes 4 cups

Ingredients:

1 small white onion, quartered
4 garlic cloves
1 bunch cilantro, with stems
1 cup fresh spinach
2 tablespoons vegetable oil
2 cups long-grain white rice, uncooked
1 teaspoon kosher salt
2 1/4 cups chicken stock

Method:

1. *Fit QuadChop bowl with blades then add the onions, garlic, cilantro and spinach.*
2. *Cover with lid and place motor on top; pulse on HIGH for 10-15 seconds or until fine; set aside.*
3. *Preheat the oil in a large saucepan over medium-high heat.*
4. *When oil is hot, add the rice and stir for 4-5 minutes to coat the rice with the oil.*
5. *Add QuadChop bowl contents and remaining ingredients to the saucepan and stir thoroughly.*
6. *Reduce heat to medium then cook until liquid is reduced just below the rice level.*
7. *Cover saucepan then reduce heat to low and cook for an additional 10 minutes.*
8. *Remove from heat and let stand for 5 minutes then fluff with a fork before serving.*

MANGO SALSA

Makes 2 cups

Ingredients:

1 mango, peeled and cut into chunks
1/4 medium red onion
3 tablespoons mango nectar
2 tablespoons fresh lime juice
1/4 cup cilantro leaves
1/2 Serrano pepper
1/2 teaspoon kosher salt
1 teaspoon granulated sugar

Method:

1. *Fit QuadChop bowl with blades then add all ingredients.*
2. *Cover with lid and place motor on top; pulse on HIGH for 5-10 seconds until chunky or until desired consistency is achieved.*
3. *Taste and adjust seasoning if desired before serving.*

TIP

This salsa can be made in advance by keeping the ingredients separate. Don't combine them until the very last minute.

GLUTEN-FREE
CORNBREAD

Makes 1 loaf

Ingredients:

1 large egg
1 1/2 cups buttermilk
1/4 cup unsalted butter, softened
1/2 cup corn kernels
2 tablespoons granulated sugar
2/3 cup cornmeal
1/2 cup rice flour
1/2 cup potato starch
2 teaspoons xanthan gum
1 1/2 teaspoons baking soda

Method:

1. Preheat oven to 375°F.
2. Fit QuadChop bowl with blades then add all ingredients.
3. Cover with lid and place motor on top; pulse on HIGH for 10-15 seconds or until fairly smooth.
4. Pour mixture into a greased 7-inch cake pan.
5. Bake in oven for 25 minutes or until well browned.
6. Remove and serve hot.

CHOCOLATE BABY CAKES

Makes 12 servings

For the Batter:
2 cups semi-sweet chocolate chips
1 1/4 cups unsalted butter
2 teaspoons instant espresso powder (optional)
8 large eggs
1 cup granulated sugar
1/4 cup all purpose flour

For the Vanilla Icing:
3 large egg whites
1 cup unsalted butter, softened
3 cups powdered sugar
1/4 teaspoon almond extract
1/4 teaspoon butter-vanilla extract
1/2 teaspoon vanilla extract
1/4 teaspoon kosher salt

Method:

1. *Preheat oven to 325°F.*
2. *In a microwave-safe bowl, combine the chocolate chips, butter and espresso if desired; microwave for 3 minutes or until chocolate has melted; remove and set aside.*
3. *Fit QuadChop bowl with blades then add the eggs and sugar.*
4. *Cover with lid and place motor on top; pulse on HIGH for 10-15 seconds or until fluffy and pale yellow in color.*
5. *Add the flour and chocolate mixture to the QuadChop bowl then pulse until mixed (do not over mix).*
6. *Pour the batter into a baby cake pan or muffin tin until each well is almost filled to the top.*
7. *Bake for 25-30 minutes or until tops look dry; remove and let cool.*
8. *Place all icing ingredients into the QuadChop bowl.*
9. *Cover with lid and place motor on top; pulse on HIGH in 5-second intervals until fluffy.*
10. *Spread the icing over the cooled baby cakes and serve.*

TIP

These cakes taste even better
when baked from a frozen state.
Freeze the dough ahead of time
for up to 2 months.

CHOCOLATE
ICE CREAM

Makes 2 cups

Ingredients:

1/2 cup heavy cream
1/3 cup powdered sugar
1/4 cup chocolate fudge sundae topping
1/2 teaspoon vanilla extract
2 cups ice cubes

Method:

1. *Fit QuadChop bowl with blades then add all ingredients.*
2. *Cover with lid and place motor on top; pulse on HIGH for 10-15 seconds or until smooth.*
3. *Use a spatula to scrape the sides of the bowl.*
4. *Cover and pulse on HIGH for an additional 5-10 seconds.*
5. *Serve immediately.*

GRAPEFRUIT TARTS

Makes 6 tarts

Ingredients:

1 tablespoon grapefruit zest
1/3 cup grapefruit juice
3 large egg yolks
1 can (14 ounces) sweetened condensed milk
6 small store-bought tart shells
Whipped cream, for serving (optional)

Method:

1. *Preheat oven to 300°F.*
2. *Fit QuadChop bowl with blades then add all ingredients, except tart shells and whipped cream.*
3. *Cover with lid and place motor on top; pulse on HIGH for 10-15 seconds or until smooth.*
4. *Divide mixture between the tart shells then place on a sheet pan.*
5. *Bake in the oven for 20-25 minutes or until just wet but still wobbly in the center.*
6. *Remove and let cool.*
7. *Chill thoroughly before serving with whipped cream if desired.*

HOMEMADE
SNO CONES

Makes 4 servings

Ingredients:
4 cups ice cubes
8 tablespoons flavored syrup (see recipes below)

Method:
1. *Fit QuadChop bowl with blades then add the ice.*
2. *Cover with lid and place motor on top; pulse on HIGH for 10-15 seconds or until ice is crushed.*
3. *Scoop crushed ice into a sno cone cup.*
4. *Top with 2 tablespoons desired syrup (see below) and serve.*

Sno Cone Syrup Ingredients:

Raspberry Syrup:
1 1/2 cups frozen raspberries
1/3 cup water
2/3 cup granulated sugar
2 tablespoons fresh lemon juice

Blueberry Syrup:
1 1/2 cups frozen blueberries
1/3 cup water
2/3 cup granulated sugar
2 tablespoons fresh lemon juice

Lime Syrup:
Zest of 2 limes
2/3 cup fresh lime juice
2/3 cup granulated sugar
1-2 drops green food coloring (optional)

Pineapple Syrup:
1 1/2 cups frozen pineapple chunks
1/3 cup water
2/3 cup granulated sugar
2 tablespoons fresh lemon juice

Syrup Method:
1. *Combine all syrup ingredients in a medium sized saucepan.*
2. *Bring to a boil over medium-high heat then remove from heat.*
3. *Pour through a fine mesh strainer into an airtight storage container.*
4. *Keep refrigerated in an airtight container for up to 1 month.*
5. *When ready to use, pour into a plastic squeeze bottle and squeeze over the crushed ice as described above.*

CHOCOLATE CRINKLE COOKIES

Makes 12 cookies

Ingredients:

1/4 cup vegetable oil
1 large egg
1 large egg yolk
1 tablespoon light corn syrup
1/2 cup semi-sweet chocolate chips, melted, slightly cooled
1 1/4 cups granulated sugar
1 teaspoon baking powder
1/4 teaspoon kosher salt
1 teaspoon vanilla extract
3/4 cup all purpose flour
Granulated sugar, for rolling
Powdered sugar, for rolling

Method:

1. *Fit QuadChop bowl with blades then add all ingredients, except flour and sugars for rolling.*
2. *Cover with lid and place motor on top; press and hold HIGH for 10-15 seconds or until smooth.*
3. *Remove the blades from the QuadChop bowl then stir in the flour using a rubber spatula.*
4. *Chill mixture for 1-2 hours.*
5. *Preheat oven to 350°F.*
6. *Line a sheet pan with parchment paper.*
7. *Use a small ice cream scoop to scoop 12 cookie dough balls.*
8. *Roll each dough ball first in granulated sugar then in powdered sugar until thoroughly coated.*
9. *Space out on the sheet pan then bake for 15 minutes or until puffed and cracked.*
10. *Remove and serve warm.*

GO GREEN SMOOTHIE

Makes 2 servings

Ingredients:

1 orange, peeled
1 fresh pineapple wedge
1 banana, peeled
1 tablespoon flax seeds
1 cup carrot juice
1 cup frozen mixed berries
1 cup frozen broccoli
2 cups frozen kale or spinach

Method:

1. *Fit QuadChop bowl with blades then add all ingredients.*
2. *Cover with lid and place motor on top; pulse on HIGH for 10-15 seconds or until smooth.*
3. *Serve immediately.*

VERY BERRY SHAKE

Makes 1 1/2 cups

Ingredients:

1 cup watermelon chunks
1 cup mixed berries
1 banana, peeled
1/4 cup whole milk
1 cup vanilla ice cream

Method:

1. *Fit QuadChop bowl with blades then add all ingredients.*
2. *Cover with lid and place motor on top; pulse on HIGH for 10-15 seconds or until smooth.*
3. *Serve immediately.*

CRISPY RICOTTA PUFFS

Makes 30 puffs

Ingredients:

7 ounces whole milk ricotta
1/3 cup granulated sugar
2 large eggs
1/4 teaspoon kosher salt
2 teaspoons vanilla extract
2 teaspoons baking powder
2 teaspoons ground cinnamon
3/4 cup all purpose flour
Canola oil, for frying
Cinnamon sugar, for rolling

Method:

1. *Fit QuadChop bowl with blades then add all ingredients, except oil for frying and cinnamon sugar.*
2. *Cover with lid and place motor on top; pulse on HIGH for 10-15 seconds or until smooth.*
3. *Pour oil into a Dutch oven until 3-inches in depth then preheat oil over medium heat to 350°F (use a clip-on thermometer to monitor temperature).*
4. *Carefully drop tablespoon-size balls of batter into the hot oil and cook for 90 seconds on each side or until golden brown.*
5. *Remove and roll balls in cinnamon sugar while still hot.*
6. *Repeat with remaining batter and serve hot.*

TIP

For a chocolate version, try adding 1/2 cup of mini chocolate chips to the batter before frying.

BUTTER PECAN MILKSHAKE

Makes 1 1/2 cups

Ingredients:

1/4 cup pecans, toasted
1/4 teaspoon maple extract
1/2 cup whole milk
2 cups vanilla ice cream
Whipped cream and additional pecans, for serving

Method:

1. *Fit QuadChop bowl with blades then add all ingredients, except whipped cream and pecans for serving.*
2. *Cover with lid and place motor on top; pulse on HIGH for 10-15 seconds or until smooth.*
3. *Serve topped with whipped cream and additional pecans.*

TIP

The extraordinary flavor in this shake comes from toasted pecans. To toast, spread pecans out on a sheet pan and place in the oven at 350°F for 15 minutes.

TROPICAL
SMOOTHIE

Makes 2 cups

Ingredients:
Zest and juice of 1 lime
1/3 cup cream of coconut
1 mango, cut into chunks, or frozen
1 banana, peeled
1/2 cup ice cubes

Method:
1. *Fit QuadChop bowl with blades then add all ingredients.*
2. *Cover with lid and place motor on top; pulse on HIGH for 10-15 seconds or until smooth.*
3. *Serve immediately.*

TIP
Don't confuse cream of coconut with coconut milk. They are not the same thing at all. Cream of coconut is thick, sweet and has an intense coconut flavor. Coconut milk is thin, unsweetened and has a subtle coconut flavor.

KIWI
SMOOTHIE

Makes 2 cups

Ingredients:

1 cup honeydew melon chunks
2 kiwis
1 banana, peeled
1 tablespoon honey
1/2 cup ice cubes

Method:

1. *Fit QuadChop bowl with blades then add all ingredients.*
2. *Cover with lid and place motor on top; pulse on HIGH for 10-15 seconds or until smooth.*
3. *Serve immediately.*

BLUEBERRY JAM

Makes 4 cups

Ingredients:

2 pints fresh blueberries
3 1/2 cups granulated sugar
2 tablespoons fresh lemon juice
1 pouch (3 ounces) liquid fruit pectin

Method:

1. *Fit QuadChop bowl with blades then add the blueberries.*
2. *Cover with lid and place motor on top; pulse on HIGH for 10-15 seconds or until fine.*
3. *Scrape 2 cups of blueberry pulp into a measuring cup.*
4. *Scrape measured pulp into a large saucepot then add remaining ingredients.*
5. *Bring to a simmer over medium heat, stirring often.*
6. *Raise heat until mixture is at a full, rolling boil then boil for 3 minutes.*
7. *Remove from heat and ladle into airtight containers; let cool completely.*
8. *Keep refrigerated in airtight containers for up to 3 months or freeze for up to 1 year.*

CHOCOLATE
MOUSSE

Makes 4 - 6 servings

Ingredients:

1 1/2 cups heavy cream
1 tablespoon granulated sugar
1/4 teaspoon vanilla extract
1/2 cup store-bought chocolate sundae topping

Method:

1. *Fit QuadChop bowl with blades then add all ingredients.*
2. *Cover with lid and place motor on top; pulse on HIGH for 10-15 seconds or until smooth.*
3. *Divide mousse between parfait glasses or bowls.*
4. *Serve immediately.*

CHOCOLATE
MILKSHAKE

Makes 2 servings

Ingredients:

4 scoops vanilla ice cream
1/2 cup store-bought chocolate sundae topping
1/2 cup half & half

Method:

1. *Fit QuadChop bowl with blades then add all ingredients.*
2. *Cover with lid and place motor on top; press and hold HIGH for 10-15 seconds or until smooth.*
3. *Serve immediately.*

CHOCOLATE CHEESECAKE DIP

Makes 1 1/2 cups

Ingredients:

1/2 cup heavy cream, very hot
1/2 cup bittersweet chocolate chips
1 package (8 ounces) cream cheese, warmed
1/3 cup powdered sugar
1 teaspoon vanilla extract

Method:

1. *Fit QuadChop bowl with blades then add the hot cream and chocolate chips.*
2. *Cover with lid and place motor on top; pulse on HIGH for 10-15 seconds or until melted.*
3. *Add remaining ingredients then pulse for an additional 10-15 seconds until uniform in color.*
4. *Serve with your choice of dippers.*

10-SECOND RASPBERRY MOUSSE

Makes 4 servings

Ingredients:

6 ounces frozen raspberries, thawed
1/3 cup granulated sugar
1 1/2 cups heavy cream
1 tablespoon granulated sugar

Method:

1. *Fit QuadChop bowl with blades then add all ingredients.*
2. *Cover with lid and place motor on top; pulse on HIGH for 10-15 seconds or until smooth.*
3. *Divide mousse between parfait glasses or bowls.*
4. *Serve immediately.*

ORANGE BREAKFAST SMOOTHIE

Makes 2 servings

Ingredients:

1 orange, peeled
1 cup frozen pineapple chunks
1 banana, peeled
1/4 cup rolled oats
1 cup plain yogurt
1 cup carrot juice

Method:

1. *Fit QuadChop bowl with blades then add all ingredients.*
2. *Cover with lid and place motor on top; pulse on HIGH for 10-15 seconds or until smooth.*
3. *Serve immediately.*

BEGINNER GREEN SMOOTHIE

Makes 2 cups

Ingredients:
1 cup spinach leaves
1 cup apple juice
1 cup pineapple chunks
2 kiwis
1 banana, peeled
1 tablespoon honey
1/2 cup frozen broccoli

Method:
1. *Fit QuadChop bowl with blades then add all ingredients.*
2. *Cover with lid and place motor on top; pulse on HIGH for 10-15 seconds or until smooth.*
3. *Serve immediately.*

STRAWBERRY
MILKSHAKE

Makes 2 servings

For the Milkshake:
1 cup strawberries, cut in half
1/4 cup granulated sugar
4 scoops vanilla ice cream
1/3 cup half & half

For the Whipped Topping:
1 cup heavy cream
2 tablespoons granulated sugar

Method:
1. *Place the strawberries and sugar in a large bowl; toss well then cover and let strawberries macerate at room temperature for 30 minutes.*
2. *Fit QuadChop bowl with blades then add all whipped topping ingredients.*
3. *Cover with lid and place motor on top; press and hold HIGH for 10-15 seconds or until smooth.*
4. *Transfer whipped topping to a small bowl.*
5. *Without cleaning the QuadChop bowl, add the strawberries and remaining milkshake ingredients.*
6. *Cover with lid and place motor on top; press and hold HIGH for 10-15 seconds or until smooth.*
7. *Pour into glasses, top with whipped topping and serve.*

TIP
Macerating the strawberries in step 1 is an important step to achieving the best flavor. The process extracts the moisture and intensifies the strawberry flavor.

MANGO LIME SORBET

Makes 2 cups

Ingredients:

2 cups frozen mango chunks
1 lime wedge with rind
1 cup orange juice

Method:

1. *Fit QuadChop bowl with blades then add all ingredients.*
2. *Cover with lid and place motor on top; pulse on HIGH for 10-15 seconds or until smooth.*
3. *Use a spatula to scrape the sides of the bowl if needed.*
4. *Repeat and pulse again on HIGH for an additional 5-10 seconds.*
5. *Serve immediately.*

POPEYE'S ICE CREAM

Makes 2 cups

Ingredients:

1 cup spinach leaves, packed
1 tablespoon fresh lemon juice
1/2 cup heavy cream
1/3 cup powdered sugar
1/2 teaspoon vanilla extract
1/4 teaspoon coconut extract
2 cups ice cubes

Method:

1. *Fit QuadChop bowl with blades then add all ingredients.*
2. *Cover with lid and place motor on top; pulse on HIGH for 10-15 seconds or until smooth.*
3. *Use a spatula to scrape the sides of the bowl if needed.*
4. *Repeat and pulse on HIGH for an additional 5-10 seconds.*
5. *Serve immediately.*

TURKEY, PASTA & ZUCCHINI
DINNER

Makes 4-6 servings

Ingredients:

1 large yellow onion, quartered
4 garlic cloves
1 celery stalk, chunked
1 pound sliced turkey breast
2 1/2 cups dry rigatoni pasta
2 1/2 cups chicken stock
1/2 cup dry white wine
1/2 cup jarred pesto sauce
Kosher salt and fresh pepper to taste
1 bag (10 ounces) frozen zucchini

Method:

1. *Fit QuadChop bowl with blades then add the onions, garlic and celery.*
2. *Cover with lid and place motor on top; pulse on HIGH for 5-10 seconds or until chunky.*
3. *Transfer QuadChop bowl contents and turkey to a large skillet over medium-high heat; stir.*
4. *Cook for 4-6 minutes or until vegetables and turkey are slightly cooked.*
5. *Add remaining ingredients, except zucchini, to the skillet; stir thoroughly.*
6. *Cover skillet then reduce heat to medium and cook for 8 minutes; stir.*
7. *Add the zucchini to the skillet; cover again and cook for an additional 8 minutes, stirring occasionally to prevent sticking.*
8. *Remove from heat and serve.*

CHICKEN & BROCCOLI SUPPER

Makes 4-6 servings

Ingredients:

1 large yellow onion, quartered
4 garlic cloves
1 carrot, chunked
1 celery stalk, chunked
1 pound chicken breast, diced
2 1/2 cups dry bow-tie pasta
2 1/2 cups chicken stock
1/2 cup dry white wine
1/2 cup whole milk
Kosher salt and fresh pepper to taste
1 bag (10 ounces) frozen broccoli

Method:

1. *Fit QuadChop bowl with blades then add the onions, garlic, carrots and celery.*
2. *Cover with lid and place motor on top; pulse on HIGH for 5-10 seconds or until roughly chopped.*
3. *Transfer QuadChop bowl contents and chicken to a large skillet over medium-high heat; stir.*
4. *Cook for 4-6 minutes or until vegetables and chicken are slightly cooked.*
5. *Add remaining ingredients, except broccoli, to the skillet; stir thoroughly.*
6. *Cover skillet then reduce heat to medium and cook for 8 minutes; stir.*
7. *Add the broccoli to the skillet; cover again and cook for an additional 8 minutes, stirring occasionally to prevent sticking.*
8. *Remove from heat and serve.*

ONE PAN VEGETARIAN PASTA

Makes 4-6 servings

Ingredients:

1 large yellow onion, quartered
1 bell pepper, quartered
4 garlic cloves
1 carrot, chunked
1 celery stalk, chunked
8 ounces dry whole wheat spaghetti
2 1/2 cups vegetable stock
1/2 cup dry white wine
1/2 cup almond milk
Kosher salt and fresh pepper to taste
1 bag (10 ounces) frozen kale, or other dark, leafy greens

Method:

1. *Fit QuadChop bowl with blades then add the onions, bell pepper, garlic, carrots and celery.*
2. *Cover with lid and place motor on top; pulse on HIGH for 5-10 seconds or until roughly chopped.*
3. *Transfer QuadChop bowl contents to a large skillet over medium-high heat; stir.*
4. *Cook for 4-6 minutes or until vegetables are slightly translucent.*
5. *Add remaining ingredients, except kale, to the skillet; stir thoroughly.*
6. *Cover skillet then reduce heat to medium and cook for 8 minutes; stir.*
7. *Add the kale to the skillet; cover again and cook for an additional 8 minutes.*
8. *Remove from heat and serve.*

TIP

This is a great recipe for using up cooked or raw vegetable leftovers from your refrigerator such as cabbage, squash, onions and tomatoes.

WALNUT
PESTO

Makes 2 cups

Ingredients:

1/2 cup fresh sage leaves
1/2 cup walnuts, toasted
Zest and juice from 1/2 of a lemon
1 teaspoon honey
3 garlic cloves
1 teaspoon kosher salt
1/2 teaspoon freshly ground pepper
1/4 cup Parmesan cheese, grated
1 cup walnut or vegetable oil

Method:

1. *Fit QuadChop bowl with blades then add all ingredients.*
2. *Cover with lid and place motor on top; press and hold HIGH for 10-15 seconds or until slightly chunky.*
3. *Taste and adjust seasoning then pour into a small serving bowl and use as desired.*
4. *Keep refrigerated in an airtight container for up to 1 week or freeze for up to 3 months.*

TIP

The walnut oil really adds a great flavor to this recipe. It can be found at most Italian markets. However, if you can't find walnut oil, it will still be delicious using vegetable oil.

WHOLE FRUIT
MARGARITA

Makes 2 servings

Ingredients:

1 orange, peeled
1 lime, peeled
1 grapefruit, peeled
1/2 cup powdered sugar
1/2 cup tequila, or to taste
1 cup ice cubes

Method:

1. *Fit QuadChop bowl with blades then add all ingredients.*
2. *Cover with lid and place motor on top; pulse on HIGH for 10-15 seconds or until smooth.*
3. *Serve immediately in salt-rimmed margarita glasses.*

EASY PANCAKES

Makes 6 pancakes

Ingredients:

2 tablespoons sour cream
1 cup buttermilk
1 large egg
1 cup unbleached all purpose flour
1/2 teaspoon kosher salt
1 tablespoon granulated sugar
1/4 teaspoon baking soda
1/2 teaspoon baking powder
Unsalted butter, for serving
Maple Syrup, for serving

Method:

1. *Preheat an electric griddle or sauté pan to 350°F.*
2. *Fit QuadChop bowl with blades then add all ingredients, except butter and maple syrup.*
3. *Cover with lid and place motor on top; pulse on HIGH for 5-10 seconds or until just combined and a few lumps remain.*
4. *Let batter rest for 5 minutes.*
5. *Ladle the batter on the griddle or sauté pan and cook for 2 minutes on each side or until brown.*
6. *Serve topped with butter and syrup.*

SWEET CREAM
PIE

Makes 1 pie

Ingredients:

3/4 cup light brown sugar, packed
1/2 cup unsalted butter, melted
1 teaspoon vanilla extract
2 tablespoons apple cider vinegar
1/4 cup buttermilk
2/3 cup heavy cream
8 large egg yolks
1/4 teaspoon kosher salt
1 store-bought frozen 9-inch pie crust, unbaked

Method:

1. *Fit QuadChop bowl with blades then add all ingredients, except pie crust.*
2. *Cover with lid and place motor on top; pulse on LOW for 10-15 seconds or until smooth.*
3. *Pour into pie crust then place in the cold oven.*
4. *Set oven temperature to 325ºF and bake pie for 50 minutes or until just set.*
5. *Remove and let cool for 1 hour before serving.*

WHOLE WHEAT PIZZA DOUGH

Makes 1 pizza dough

Ingredients:

1/2 cup water
1 tablespoon olive oil
1 teaspoon honey
1 teaspoon kosher salt
1 cup whole wheat flour
2 teaspoons active dry yeast
1 teaspoon onion powder (optional)
1 teaspoon Italian seasoning (optional)

Method:

1. *Fit QuadChop bowl with blades then add all ingredients.*
2. *Cover with lid and place motor on top; press and hold HIGH for 10-15 seconds or until a dough ball forms.*
3. *Let dough rest for 30 minutes then pulse on HIGH for an additional 10-15 seconds.*
4. *Shape dough into a smooth ball and use as desired.*
5. *Dough can be kept in an airtight container in the freezer for up to 2 months.*

TIP

To use this dough to make a whole wheat pizza, flatbread or foccacia, roll out the dough ball to desired shape, cover and let rest for 30 minutes, top as desired and bake in the oven at 450°F for 10-15 minutes or until well browned.

ORANGE
MARMALADE

Makes 4 cups

Ingredients:

4-5 oranges, quartered
3 cups granulated sugar
1 box (1.75 ounces) dry fruit pectin

Method:

1. *Fit QuadChop bowl with blades then add the oranges.*
2. *Cover with lid and place motor on top; pulse on HIGH for 10-15 seconds or until fine.*
3. *Transfer 1 1/2 cups of orange pulp from the QuadChop bowl to a measuring cup.*
4. *Scrape measured pulp into a large saucepot then add remaining ingredients (save extra pulp for another use or discard).*
5. *Bring to a simmer over medium heat, stirring often.*
6. *Raise heat until mixture is at a full, rolling boil then boil for 3 minutes.*
7. *Remove from heat and ladle into airtight containers; let cool and use as desired.*
8. *Keep refrigerated in airtight containers for up to 3 months or freeze for up to 1 year.*

FRUIT OR VEGETABLE
BABY FOODS

Makes 2 - 4 servings

For Fruits:

1 cup fresh or frozen fruit of choice, preferably organic
1/4 cup water, juice or formula

For Vegetables:

1 cup diced vegetable of choice, preferably organic, steamed until tender
1/4 cup water, juice or formula

Method:

1. Fit QuadChop bowl with blades then add all fruit or vegetable ingredients.
2. Cover with lid and place motor on top; pulse on HIGH for 10-15 seconds or until smooth.
3. Use a spatula to scrape the sides of the bowl then pulse on HIGH for an additional 10-15 seconds.
4. If a smoother texture is desired, push the baby food through a fine mesh strainer.
5. Serve immediately.
6. Keep refrigerated in an airtight container for up to 2 days or freeze for up to 1 month.

FRUIT SMOOTHIE

Makes 2 cups

Ingredients:

8 large strawberries
2 apricots
1 banana, peeled
1/4 cup plain yogurt
1 tablespoon honey
1/2 cup ice cubes

Method:

1. *Fit QuadChop bowl with blades then add all ingredients.*
2. *Cover with lid and place motor on top; pulse on HIGH for 10-15 seconds or until smooth.*
3. *Serve immediately.*

STEALTH HEALTH
SMOOTHIE

Makes 2 servings

Ingredients:

1 cup frozen raspberries
1 small beet, quartered
1/2 cucumber, chunked
1 fresh pineapple wedge
1 banana, peeled
1 tablespoon flax or chia seeds
1 cup pomegranate juice
2 cups frozen kale or spinach

Method:

1. *Fit QuadChop bowl with blades then add all ingredients.*
2. *Cover with lid and place motor on top; pulse on HIGH for 10-15 seconds or until smooth.*
3. *Serve immediately.*

FUN
SLIME

NOTE: THIS IS NOT FOR HUMAN CONSUMPTION!

Ingredients:

1/2 cup water
1/4 cup white school-type glue
1 tablespoon talcum powder, such as baby powder
A few drops of desired food coloring
1 tablespoon borax powder (found near the laundry detergent in most grocery stores)

Method:

1. *Fit QuadChop bowl with blades then add all ingredients.*
2. *Cover with lid and place motor on top; pulse on HIGH for 10-15 seconds or until thickened.*
3. *Thin with more water if desired before using.*
4. *Store in an airtight container when children are not playing with it.*

TIP

When the Slime gets dried out from play, place it back in the QuadChop and add a small amount of water then pulse until desired texture is achieved again.

SOURCE PAGE

Here are some of my favorite places to find ingredients that are not readily available at grocery stores as well as kitchen tools and supplies that help you become a better cook.

The Bakers Catalogue at King Arthur Flour

135 Route 5 South
P.O. Box 1010
Norwich, VT 05055

Pure fruit oils, citric acid, silicone spatulas, digital timers, oven thermometers, real truffle oil, off-set spatulas, measuring cups and spoons, knives, ice cream scoops, cheesecloth, cookie sheets, baking pans
www.kingarthurflour.com

Chocosphere

P.O. Box 2237
Tualatin, OR 97062
877-992-4623

Excellent quality cocoa (Callebaut)
All Chocolates
Jimmies and sprinkles
www.chocosphere.com

Gluten Free Mall

4927 Sonoma HWY Suite C1
Santa Rosa, CA 95409
707-509-4528

All ingredients needed for gluten-free baking
www.glutenfreemall.com

Vanilla From Tahiti

Nui Enterprises
501 Chapala St. Suite A
Santa Barbara, CA 93101
805-965-5153
www.vanillafromtahiti.com

D & G Occasions

625 Herndon Ave.
Orlando, FL 32803
407-894-4458

My favorite butter vanilla extract by Magic Line, cake and candy making supplies, citric acid, pure fruit oils, professional food colorings, ultra thin flexible spatulas, large selection of sprinkles and jimmies, unusual birthday candles, pure vanilla extract, pastry bags and tips, parchment, off-set spatulas, oven and candy thermometers, kitchen timers, meat mallets, large selection of cookie cutters
www.dandgoccasions.com

Penzeys Spices

P.O. Box 924
Brookfield, WI 53045
800-741-7787

Spices, extracts, seasonings, seasonal cookie cutters, mallets and more
www.penzeys.com

INDEX

INDEX

111

FOR ALL OF MARIAN GETZ'S COOKBOOKS AS WELL AS
COOKWARE, APPLIANCES, CUTLERY AND KITCHEN ACCESSORIES
BY WOLFGANG PUCK

PLEASE VISIT HSN.COM
(KEYWORD: WOLFGANG PUCK)